History of America

BUILDING AN EMPIRE:
The Louisiana Purchase

Written by Linda Thompson

Rourke
Educational Media

rourkeeducationalmedia.com

www.rourkeeducationalmedia.com

PHOTO CREDITS:
Courtesy Butch Bouvier, www.keelboat.com: page 33; Courtesy Charles Reasoner: pages 16, 35; Courtesy Independence National Historic Park: pages 25, 26; Courtesy Library of Congress, Edward S. Curtis Collection: pages 31, 37, 38; Courtesy Library of Congress Prints and Photographs Division: Title Page, pages 5, 7, 8, 9, 10, 11, 12, 17, 18, 19, 20, 23, 24, 28, 29, 34, 42; Courtesy National Archives and Records Administration: pages 22, 30, Courtesy National Parks Service: pages 6, 39, 43; Courtesy Rohm Padilla: pages 4, 13, 27; Courtesy U.S. Army, Center of Military History: page 15; Courtesy U.S. Senate Archives: 21, 40; Courtesy U.S. Fish and Wildlife Service: pages 40, 41; Courtesy USGS: page 36.

Edited by Jill Sherman

Cover design by Nicola Stratford, bdpublishing.com

Interior layout by Tara Raymo

Library of Congress PCN Data

Thompson, Linda
Building an Empire: The Louisiana Purchase / Linda Thompson.
ISBN 978-1-62169-842-5 (hard cover)
ISBN 978-1-62169-737-4 (soft cover)
ISBN 978-1-62169-946-0 (e-Book)
Library of Congress Control Number: 2013936393

Also Available as:
ROURKE'S e-Books

Rourke Educational Media
Printed in the United States of America,
North Mankato, Minnesota

Rourke

rourkeeducationalmedia.com

customerservice@rourkeeducationalmedia.com • PO Box 643328 Vero Beach, Florida 32964

TABLE OF CONTENTS

Chapter 1

LOUISIANA: THE NEW TERRITORY

Only 20 years after it became independent, the United States suddenly and owing to a tremendous stroke of luck doubled in size. Fifty years later, the young country stretched across immense plains and towering mountain ranges to touch the Pacific Ocean. How it grew so fast in such a short time is still an amazing tale.

Thomas Jefferson (1743-1826) was the third President of the United States.

By far the largest growth spurt of the United States occurred in 1803, when President Thomas Jefferson's bold decision doubled the country's size. The Louisiana Purchase, the new **territory** acquired by the U.S., reached from the Mississippi River to the Rocky Mountains, a total of about 828,00 square miles (2,144,354 square kilometers) of land.

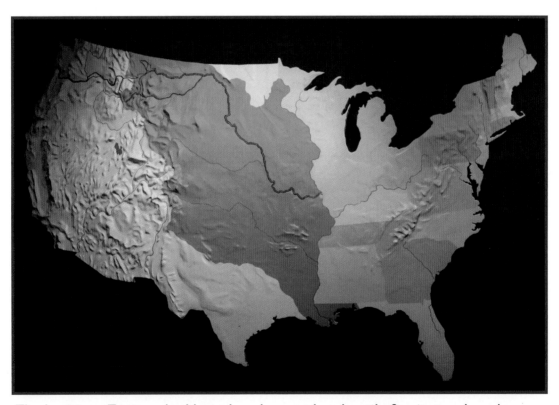

The Louisiana Territory had been largely unexplored until after its purchase by the United States.

At the start of the nineteenth century, the United States had only 17 states and the large Northwest Territory, which surrounded the Great Lakes. There were five and a half million Americans, mostly living along the eastern **seaboard**. However, more than 700,000 settlers moved west of the Appalachian Mountains after the American Revolution ended in 1783. They pressed into regions that later became Ohio, Indiana, Illinois, Kentucky, Tennessee, Alabama, and Mississippi. These people, who by 1803 outnumbered Native Americans by eight to one, were farmers, fur traders, hunters, and adventurers. Many of them used the Mississippi River and the vital port of New Orleans to send their products to the Atlantic coast and to Europe.

But the lower Mississippi and New Orleans remained in foreign hands. Originally claimed in the name of King Louis XIV by French explorers in 1682, Louisiana had been under Spanish control since 1763. Winning the American Revolution had given the United States the Northwest Territory, while Britain retained

King Louis XIV (1638-1715)

Canada and continued to claim Oregon Country. However, Spain still controlled Florida, the Southwest, and all of the land from Texas to the Pacific Ocean.

The Proclamation of 1763 declared that the colonies could not build west of the Appalachian Mountains, which changed after the American Revolution.

Although Spain had been an American ally in the Revolution, Spain was determined to keep Americans out of its territory. In particular, the sparsely populated lands west of the Mississippi River made an excellent buffer zone between Spain's rich silver mines in Mexico and the restless Americans, who always seemed to want more land.

Americans living near the **frontier** often felt neglected by their government. Some politicians in remote areas began encouraging groups of people to **secede** from the United States and become a part of Spain. Congress now had to decide whether to encourage or discourage western settlement, and in 1787 it passed the Northwest Ordinance. This act said that settlers could elect a territorial government when 5,000 males, not including slaves, lived in a district, and with 60,000 people, they could apply for statehood.

Thomas Jefferson suggested many names for new states such as Metropotamia, Pelisipia, and Slyvania.

The Declaration of Independence was outlined by Thomas Jefferson, John Adams, and Benjamin Franklin, and written by Jefferson.

The men that fought for the United States were called Patriots.

THE AMERICAN REVOLUTION

After the wars with France, England was left with a growing empire and a huge debt, so the king of England raised taxes in the American colonies. Colonists protested the new taxes and began to form militia groups. The American Revolutionary War began in 1775, and on July 4, 1776, the Second Continental Congress adopted the Declaration of Independence. The British surrendered in 1781, and the Treaty of Paris, signed on September 3, 1783, granted the 13 colonies independence.

Before the Civil War, New Orleans had the largest population of free blacks in the South. At trade schools like this one, free blacks could learn useful skills to make a living.

Throughout its colonial history, New Orleans and the surrounding land had been unique. It had a large African population, mostly from one region in West Africa. Many black individuals were not slaves, but free tradesmen. By 1795, about half of New Orleans' carpenters, joiners, shoemakers, silversmiths, gunsmiths, and seamstresses were free blacks. Native Americans also made up a large segment of the population throughout the eighteenth century, and they shared food, medicines, and other trade goods with colonists, teaching them Native American building methods and games. After the Revolution, New Orleans became a regional trade center, with many shops and market stalls throughout the city. Because both France and Spain had colonies in the West Indies and sent spices, tobacco, sugar, and slaves to America through New Orleans, that city had a mix of people, cultures, and languages unlike any other place in the country.

THE CAJUNS

Louisiana has long been the home of Cajuns, descendants of French-speaking immigrants who were forced to leave Nova Scotia, Canada, in the mid-1700s. The word *cajun* comes from Acadian, or people of Acadia, an early name of Nova Scotia. The British forced them into boats, and they wandered for years, eventually finding themselves welcomed by the Spanish authorities of Louisiana. Today, about 85,000 Americans consider themselves Cajuns, and 45,000 of them live in Louisiana. They are especially known for Cajun cooking, music, and dance.

Cajun food tends to be made with seafood that incorporates blends of spices to make healthy, delicious meals.

In 1763, Louis XIV's **successor**, Louis XV, had given New Orleans and the surrounding mass of land to his cousin, Carlos III of Spain. Always suspicious of large numbers of newcomers moving into its territory, Spain closed New Orleans and the lower Mississippi to foreigners in 1784. But 11 years later concerned that the powerful Great Britain might try to seize Louisiana, Spain signed Pinckney's Treaty with the United States, assuring Americans of the right to navigate the Lower Mississippi and establishing New Orleans as a duty-free port.

Meanwhile, the French Revolution, which began in 1789, had produced a powerful general, Napoleon Bonaparte. Napoleon eventually became emperor of France and conquered territory all over Europe. Americans suspected that Napoleon also had ambitions in the New World.

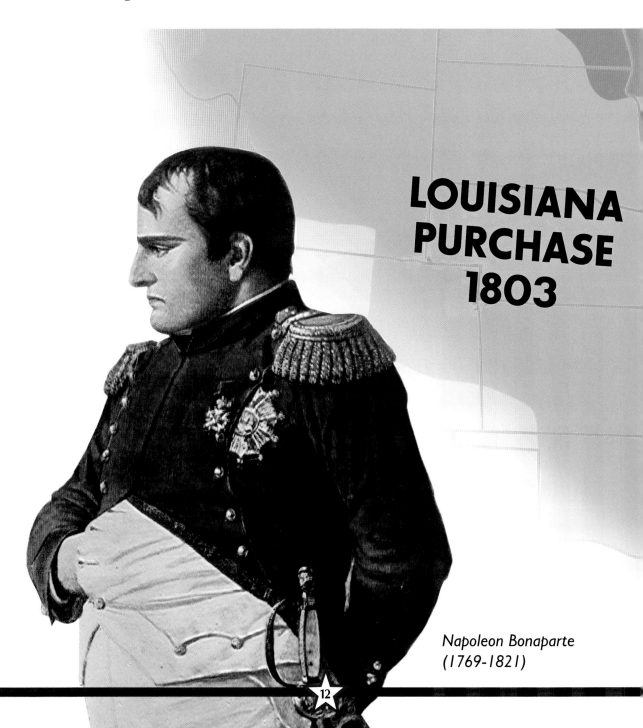

LOUISIANA PURCHASE 1803

Napoleon Bonaparte (1769-1821)

LOUISIANA THEN AND NOW

Louisiana was the name of the huge territory that President Jefferson bought. Its vast wilderness reached from the Gulf of Mexico to Canada and from the Mississippi River to the Rocky Mountains. Today, that territory makes up 15 different states: Arkansas, Colorado, Iowa, Kansas, Louisiana, Minnesota, Missouri, Montana, Nebraska, New Mexico, North Dakota, Oklahoma, South Dakota, Texas, and Wyoming. The portion of the Louisiana territory that makes up today's Louisiana was called the Territory of Orleans. The boot-shaped territory was admitted as a state in 1812 and renamed Louisiana.

STATE OF LOUISIANA

Chapter 2

NAPOLEON'S SECRET TREATY WITH SPAIN

Hoping to reconquer the French West Indies, much of which had been lost in the 1790s through colonist revolts, Napoleon saw New Orleans as a convenient port for supplying the West Indies with food and timber. Napoleon offered the queen of Spain, Maria Luisa, a kingdom called Etruria in Tuscany, Italy, in exchange for Louisiana. The queen was excited because she had grown up in Etruria. Her husband, King Carlos IV, was also thrilled because trying to govern Louisiana had been draining the Spanish treasury. This would be a good way to retain the buffer zone protecting the Mexican colony from the United States while having France bear the cost.

Flag of Spain

Flag of France

Spain and France formalized the transfer of Louisiana through the secret Treaty of San Ildefonso in 1800. Secrecy was necessary because if the Americans learned of the deal they might attack Spain's weak forces in New Orleans. It would be to America's advantage to do that instead of waiting until France, a much more powerful country, controlled New Orleans.

In 1801, the newly elected president, Thomas Jefferson, was alarmed to hear that the port of New Orleans might be back in French hands. If this rumor were true, he said, "it would be impossible that France and the United States can continue long as friends." On October 15, 1801 he assigned his friend, Robert Livingston, to be the American Minister to France. Livingston's mission was to discourage Napoleon from damaging relations with the United States by acquiring Louisiana.

SECRET AGENT NO. 13

James Wilkinson, a friend of Jefferson, had secretly signed on with Spanish officials in New Orleans to become a spy for Spain. He was called "secret agent No. 13" and had a salary of $2,000 a year. He

advised Spain to encourage American settlement of Louisiana in the early 1790s. Secretary of State Jefferson wrote in enthusiasm, "I wish a hundred thousand of our inhabitants would accept the invitation. It will be the means of delivery to us peaceably, what may otherwise cost us a war."

James Wilkinson (1757-1825)

General Toussaint L'Ouverture (1743–1803)

Livingston tried his best, but the French kept denying that they had a treaty with Spain concerning Louisiana. Meanwhile, Livingston learned that thousands of French troops were on their way to St. Dominigue, now Haiti, a French colony that had rebelled. A former slave, General Toussaint L'Ouverture, was in charge. Napoleon wanted to retake that island because of its valuable sugar crop.

THOMAS JEFFERSON

Thomas Jefferson was probably the best educated of early American presidents. He graduated from William and Mary College in Virginia and then studied law. Well-read in science, agriculture, and political history, he was a successful lawyer until drawn into politics as the first Secretary of State under President Washington. He was a skilled architect, designing his own home, Monticello. He died on July 4, 1826, the 50th anniversary of the

Declaration of Independence. He wanted to be remembered as the author of the Declaration of Independence, the founder of the University of Virginia, and a fighter for religious freedom.

Thomas Jefferson's plantation home, Monticello, is located in Virginia. Today, it is pictured on the back of the U.S. nickel.

YELLOW FEVER

Yellow fever was a widespread disease in the eighteenth and nineteenth centuries. For a long time, people thought the disease was carried

by the air. In a way it was. Yellow fever is transmitted by mosquitoes. Cities located near marshes or swamps often had yellow fever outbreaks. Thousands of people died from yellow fever.

The yellow fever epidemic peaked in New Orleans during the years 1833 and 1853.

Livingston asked Napoleon to cede New Orleans to the United States, promising that the port would remain duty-free to French ships, but Napoleon was not interested. Instead, he ordered his naval minister to prepare to take Louisiana by force in case the Americans should resist. But the minister could not form a fleet because most French ships had already sailed for St. Domingue. Unknown to Napoleon, large numbers of his troops were being wiped out by Toussaint's forces, as well as by yellow fever.

JEFFERSON TO LIVINGSTON

"There is on the globe one spot the possessor of which is our natural… enemy. It is New Orleans, through which the produce of three-eighths of our territory must pass to market. The day that France takes possession of New Orleans… we must marry ourselves to the British fleet and nation."

Robert Livingston (1787-1856)

On October 16, 1802, the Spanish governor of Louisiana suddenly banned American traders from storing cargo at New Orleans. This effectively closed the port once more to American ships. Citizens and politicians were outraged and began talking about sending troops to seize New Orleans. Realizing he had to act, in March 1803 Jefferson sent James Monroe to France as **envoy** extraordinary to help Livingston with his negotiations.

James Monroe (1758-1831)

The French only controlled New Orleans for two years before it was purchased by the United States under the Louisiana Purchase in 1803.

Monroe was a popular diplomat who had served with George Washington at Valley Forge. Jefferson instructed him to attempt to buy New Orleans and western Florida for $9,375,000. Jefferson and others believed Florida to be under French control but it actually belonged to Spain. If Monroe's offer was rejected, he was to offer $7.5 million for New Orleans alone. And if Napoleon refused, Monroe was to try to obtain the permanent right of Americans to use the lower Mississippi River and store their wares in New Orleans.

HOW MUCH IN TODAY'S DOLLARS?

Monroe intended to offer $9,375,000 ($151.7 million in today's dollars) for New Orleans and western Florida or $7.5 million ($121.4 million today) for New Orleans alone. France's initial offer for all of Louisiana was $22,500,000 ($364.07 million in today's dollars). The final price? Fifteen million in 1803, which would amount to $242.7 million if the deal were made today.

If Monroe could not achieve any of these goals, Jefferson was prepared to form an alliance with Great Britain and try to take Louisiana by force. The President wrote that "the future destinies of this republic depended on Monroe's mission succeeding."

A few months before Monroe sailed Napoleon learned of his disastrous losses in St. Domingue. Of 28,300 troops sent in 1802, by September of that year, only 4,000 remained fit for service.

With the Constitution of 1802, Toussaint, a leader of the St. Domingue revolution, abolished slavery of the entire island of St. Domingue.

Also, a new war was looming with Britain, and the French treasury was badly in need of cash. Napoleon's priority was to preserve and expand his European empire. Therefore, during the spring of 1803 he decided to sell all of Louisiana to the United States. In an amazing about-face, he told his advisers, "I already consider the Colony as completely lost,

François de Barbé-Marbois (1745-1837)

and it seems to me that in the hands of [the United States] it will be more useful to France than if I should try to keep it." He directed his minister of finance, François de Barbé-Marbois, to negotiate with Livingston. Smugly, Napoleon wrote, "This accession of territory strengthens forever the power of the United States and I have just given to England a maritime rival that sooner or later will humble her pride."

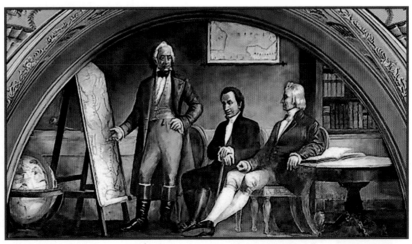

Livingston and Monroe negotiating with Barbé-Marbois.

France offered the entire territory of Louisiana for $22,500,000. Livingston at first was unprepared, replying that the United States was only interested in New Orleans and Florida. Monroe had just arrived but was confined to bed with painful backaches, so Livingston had to negotiate alone. On April 27, Livingston and Barbé-Marbois appeared in Monroe's room with the news that Napoleon had lowered his price to $16 million. Monroe and Livingston countered with $12 million, though technically they were operating well beyond their authority. In the final treaty, signed on May 2, 1803, the two ministers agreed to pay $15 million for a chunk of wilderness, the size and extent of which were pretty much undefined.

The signed Louisiana Purchase made it to Washington, D.C. on July 4, 1803.

NAPOLEON'S WORDS

"Louisiana, its territory, and the dependencies appertaining thereto, shall become part of the American Union and shall constitute in due course one or several States according to the terms of the Constitution of the

United States… The United States undertake to favor in a special way the commerce and navigation of French citizens… French and Spanish vessels and merchandise shall never be subjected to any of the customs or duties which may be imposed upon the commerce of other nations."

—Napoleon's Order for the Sale of Louisiana, April 23, 1803.

Napoleon Bonaparte (1769-1821)

To make sure it reached the United States, couriers carried copies of the treaty on three separate ships. Yet it was nearly two and a half months before President Jefferson got the news, with the first ship docking on July 14. When he realized what his envoys had accomplished, an elated Jefferson called the purchase "a transaction replete with blessings to unborn millions of men."

Chapter 3

THOMAS JEFFERSON'S DREAM

Long before he became President of the United States, Thomas Jefferson dreamed of the West. Although Jefferson himself had not ventured into the frontier lands, he had always imagined that Americans would someday find the fabled Great River of the West, or Northwest Passage, that would lead to the Pacific Ocean. While he was Secretary of State and even before, he had sought the perfect adventurer who could fulfill this dream.

The government mission would eventually lead to Kettle Falls on the Columbia River, Stevens County, Washington.

After he was elected president, Jefferson's attention turned to a young man, Meriwether Lewis, whom he had known as a neighbor in Albemarle County, Virginia. Lewis had six years of Army service on the frontier and President Jefferson thought he would be ideal for a mission to explore the uncharted West. He offered Lewis the position of personal secretary to the president. Lewis, who was at the time paymaster for the First United States Infantry Regiment, quickly accepted.

President Thomas Jefferson (1743-1826)

Meriwether Lewis (1774-1809)

William Clark (1770-1838)

From the start, Jefferson and Lewis discussed an expedition to the Pacific. By 1802, Lewis had begun collecting equipment and estimating the costs of such a journey. The two planned it as a peaceful scientific investigation so as not to alarm the Spanish or the French, into whose territory the explorers would be heading. Lewis ordered knives, rifles, and ammunition and began supervising the construction of an iron frame for a boat, which he named *The Experiment*. He began taking lessons in **celestial navigation** and consulted a physician about how to care for his men in the back country.

On January 18, 1803, Jefferson quietly sought funding from Congress to pay for an expedition to explore the West. He described it as a literary pursuit but also tempted Congress by referring to the great supplies of furs that England was acquiring from Native Americans along the Missouri River. Congress approved $2,500 for his plan.

The route Lewis and Clark took from the Atlantic to the Pacific Ocean in their exploration of North America.

When the news reached the White House on July 14 that Louisiana now belonged to the United States, the need for secrecy vanished. A month before, Lewis had written to William Clark, with whom he had served on the frontier, asking him to co-lead the expedition. Clark was the brother of a Revolutionary War hero, George Rogers Clark. William happily replied, "My friend I do assure you that no man lives with whom I would prefer to undertake such a trip as yourself." In September the two met at Louisville, Kentucky, where they recruited volunteers and began assembling their gear. They traveled down the Ohio River to the Mississippi and then upriver to St. Louis, Missouri, where they set up winter camp.

William Claiborne (1600-1677)

Meanwhile, Spain was not at all happy about the sale of Louisiana to the United States. The promised exchange of the colony for the kingdom of Etruria had never come to pass. Now, Napoleon had sold land that, in Spanish eyes, still belonged to Spain. The Spanish minister in New Orleans prepared to defend it against an American takeover. But when Jefferson threatened to take both Louisiana and Florida by force, Spain backed down. King Carlos IV ordered his officials to transfer Louisiana to France.

On November 30, 1803, the Spanish governor placed the keys to New Orleans's forts on a silver platter and handed them to French commissioner Pierre Laussat. Only 20 days later, Laussat, who had hoped to preside over a French Louisiana, stood on a hotel balcony with tears in his eyes, as he handed the keys to William Claiborne, Governor of Mississippi, and James Wilkinson who was now Commanding General of the U.S. Army. The French flag was promptly lowered. It would never again fly over any colony on the continent of North America.

Reactions to the Louisiana Purchase in the United States varied from wild enthusiasm to angry protest. The **Federalists** felt that $15 million was a foolish price to pay for "a wilderness unpeopled with any beings except wolves and wandering Indians," in the words of one newspaper editor. The Constitution did not

The American flag is raised in New Orleans.

provide for a president to acquire new land, and some felt that the purchase was illegal.

Jefferson's promise of citizenship to people living outside the United States was also questioned. In case the treaty should be challenged, Jefferson drafted a constitutional amendment that said, "Louisiana, as ceded by France to the United States, is made part of the United States." But hearing that Napoleon might be regretting the sale, he decided to rush the treaty to the Senate instead of pursuing an amendment. It took only four days for the Senate to **ratify** the treaty, and on October 20, 1803, Louisiana became American land.

HOW THE U.S. PAID FOR IT

In 1803, the U.S. had a debt of $7,852,000 and no cash. Napoleon's Minister of Finance, François de Barbé-Marbois, who had arranged the deal with Livingston, offered help. He arranged for a British bank to lend the U.S. the $15 million. Although England was at war with France, the English prime minister approved the loan. He was eager to get France out of North America. The British bank paid Napoleon cash and then exchanged Louisiana for U.S. **bonds** worth $15 million. They would be paid back with dividends, at six percent **interest**, within 15 years.

Receipt signed by Robert Livingston as part of the transaction.

The purchase treaty did not define the exact limits of the new territory. The only boundaries the French had recognized were those existing when Spain owned the colony, and they were very vaguely defined. Especially near Texas and New Mexico, the boundaries were unclear. Some critics feared that settlers in the huge land would be so scattered that they would be ungovernable. Also, they felt that the unknown Native groups in Louisiana might resist American settlers.

Native groups such as the Atsina were unknown to settlers.

Spain and the United States could not agree on Louisiana's western border with Texas, which was a part of Spanish-owned Mexico. Attempts to resolve the question broke down in 1805, when the two countries broke off diplomatic relations. General Wilkinson found a solution acceptable to both sides, in part because he was still on Spain's payroll as a spy. His compromise established a neutral strip of land, with a 10-year period during which neither power would be in charge. In 1819, both countries signed a treaty that placed the boundary along the Sabine River, where it remains today.

Chapter 4

THE LEWIS AND CLARK EXPEDITION

Like many people of the time, Thomas Jefferson believed that a river must run westward from the Missouri to the Pacific Ocean. A main goal of the Lewis and Clark expedition, officially known as the Corps of Discovery, was to find this Northwest Passage.

Captain Meriwether Lewis was 30 years old. Lieutenant William Clark was 34. About 45 men, young explorers, soldiers, and French river guides, made up their expedition. Clark took along his African-American slave named York, who he always referred to as his servant. Also accompanying the group was Lewis's black Newfoundland dog, Seaman. On May 14, 1804, the Corps set out up the Missouri River in a large **keelboat** and two pirogues. The soldiers rode along the banks to hunt and to guard against Native American attacks. In case there was no connecting river, Lewis carried wheels and axles for building carts and carrying supplies overland. They sailed, rowed, or poled the keelboat or pulled it from shore with ropes. They were able to travel about 14 miles (22.5 kilometers) on a good day.

A keelboat is a long, narrow boat designed to travel down rivers and through shallow waters.

The ships cargo included things like medicine, flags, weapons, and gifts for peoples they may encounter.

After traveling for 164 days and about 1,600 miles (2,575 kilometers), the Corps came to the villages of the friendly Mandan tribe, near what is now Bismarck, North Dakota. It was winter, so they made their camp there. It was a lucky decision because they met a French-Indian, Toussaint Charbonneau, whose 18-year-old wife was to be of great importance to their journey. Her name was Sacagawea, which means "Bird Woman." As a child, she had been stolen from her Shoshone family in western Montana, and she remembered her homeland well. She could speak various Native American languages as well as French. Since her husband could speak both French and English, Lewis and Clark conversed with Sacagawea through him. Getting this couple to accompany them to the Pacific as **interpreters** turned out to be a wise move, contributing to the success of the expedition.

During the time Lewis and Clark visited the Mandan people, the population had greatly decreased from nine to two villages because of smallpox and war.

SACAGAWEA'S BABY

Sacagawea carried her two-month-old infant, Jean Baptiste Charbonneau, on a cradleboard. William Clark was fond of the baby and called him Pompy, or Pomp. Clark later took charge of the boy's education. Baptiste spent six years in Europe as the guest of a German prince and became fluent in four languages. As an adult, he was a mountain man, scout, and trapper, even participating in the California Gold Rush.

Sacagawea (1788-1812)

Great Falls had been completely unseen by European or American eyes until Lewis and Clark.

The Corps of Discovery reached the Great Falls of the Missouri River in June 1805. It took them two more months to reach the river's **headwaters** at the present Montana-Idaho boundary. Part of this journey was made on the river, and much of it had to be made by **portage**, carrying supplies overland. Sacagawea recognized some of the country of her childhood, and on August 21, when they reached the top of the Continental Divide, they met a Shoshone band on horseback. Sacagawea burst into tears when she saw that her brother, Chief Cameahwait, was leading the band. The Shoshone supplied the Corps with horses and guided them for some miles.

Lewis and Clark reached Decision Point, the joining place of the Missouri and Marias rivers, before coming to Great Falls.

Three weeks later, the explorers found themselves in trouble. Lost and without game, they had to kill and eat some of their horses. But finally they reached the Clearwater River near present-day Orofino, Idaho. This was the homeland of the Nez Percé tribe, who were friendly and greatly helpful to Lewis and Clark. The tribe fed the explorers and helped them build canoes made of hollowed-out tree trunks. They agreed to watch over their horses, and on October 7, 1805, the Corps set off down the Clearwater in several log canoes. One month later, by connecting first with the Snake River and then with the Columbia, they had reached the Pacific Ocean. They built Fort Clatsop a few miles south of the Columbia's **mouth**, and spent the winter there.

Lewis and Clark even left their horses with the Nez Percé people to be taken care of as they traveled the rest of the way to the Pacific Ocean.

On the return trip, the Corps divided in half near present-day Missoula, Montana. Lewis led his party north up the Clark's Fork River to reach Great Falls, and Clark led the rest of the men in exploring the Yellowstone River to the south. Lewis's trip took much less time than expected, so before meeting up with Clark he decided to investigate the plains country to the north and west. But in doing so, he met a band of Blackfoot, the most powerful and warlike tribe in the Northwest. The Blackfoot tried to steal some of the party's guns and horses at dawn. Lewis's party killed one warrior and wounded another. The incident marked the first act of bloodshed between the western Indians and representatives of the United States.

The incident with the Blackfoot angered the tribe and made the country around the upper Missouri and Yellowstone rivers dangerous for travelers for many years afterward.

On his way to join Clark, Lewis was wounded by a member of his party while they were hunting elk. Although he was in pain, Lewis led the group to the Missouri, where they built boats and met Clark's party as planned. Leaving Charbonneau, Sacagawea, and her baby at the Mandan villages, the Corps of Discovery returned to St. Louis on September 23, 1806. They had traveled more than 8,000 miles (12,875 kilometers) in two years, four months, and ten days. About half of their crew had completed the entire trip, while the other half had returned at mid-point to carry maps and scientific samples back to President Jefferson.

NEW SPECIES DISCOVERED

Lewis and Clark filled a dozen elk-skin notebooks with journals and sketches. They scientifically documented 178 plant species and 122 animal species for the first time. New plants included bitterroot, bear grass, Oregon grape, salal, and salmonberry. Some animals were sent to Jefferson alive, including a prairie dog and four magpies. Others were shipped as remains: elk antlers, the skin and bones of a badger, the hide of a weasel, and a painted buffalo robe from the Mandan tribe. Among the creatures identified for the first time were the harbor seal, California condor, bighorn sheep, mountain goat, cutthroat trout, sage grouse, Steller's jay, mountain lion, grizzly bear, pronghorn, mule deer, Western gull, raccoon, coyote, and pocket gopher. Some of the plant and animal species were named after the expedition's leaders, such as Clark's nutcracker and Lewis's woodpecker.

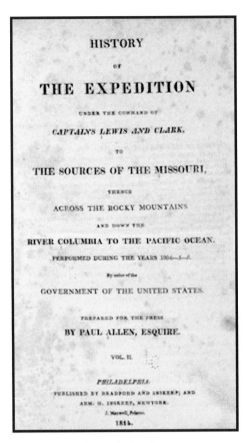

Title page from a book reporting on the Lewis and Clark expedition.

The Corps of Discovery found no Northwest Passage, but it did help establish the presence of the United States in the Pacific Northwest. Lewis and Clark compiled an astounding encyclopedia of the land, plants, wildlife, weather, and Native peoples in this largely unexplored territory. The Corps mapped thousands of miles of unexplored land, setting the stage for exploration and settlement of the Louisiana Territory. They made friends with many Native American groups, though the Blackfoot were an exception, and noted and sketched hundreds of details of their lives. They accomplished all of this for a final cost of $38,727. In gratitude, Congress doubled the pay of every member of the Corps, and gave them each 320 acres (130 hectares) of land. Lewis and Clark received 1,600 acres (648 hectares) of land and further government commissions. Charbonneau was also paid, but Sacagawea received nothing.

Published eight years after they returned, the journals of Lewis and Clark represent an impressive accomplishment, even today. Despite many hardships, only one man died during the entire expedition, Charles Floyd, who became ill in Iowa. Many historic landmarks have been placed along the route to help people trace the Corps's journey and understand its significance.

A monument was established in Iowa at the grave of Charles Floyd.

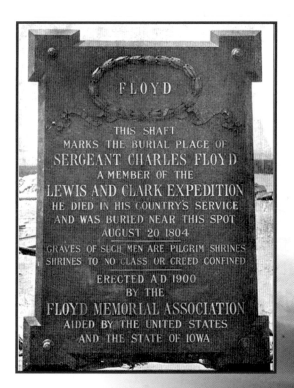

BIOGRAPHIES

Many people played important roles throughout this time period. Learn more about them in the Biographies section.

Louis XIV (1638-1715) - King of France (1643-1715), for whom Louisiana was named in 1682.

Carlos III (1716-1788) - King of Spain (1759-1788), who gained Louisiana from France in 1763.

Toussaint L'Ouverture, François Dominigue (1744-1803) - Independence leader of St. Domingue (Haiti); although he defeated Napoleon's troops on the island, he was captured and died in a French prison.

Barbé-Marbois, François de (1745-1837) - French Minister of Finance under Napoleon.

Livingston, Robert (1746-1813) - U.S. diplomat who helped negotiate the Louisiana Purchase.

Monroe, James (1758-1831) - Fifth president of the United States (1817-1825); with Robert Livingston, negotiated the Louisiana Purchase in 1803.

Charbonneau, Toussaint (1767-1843) - French-Indian husband of Sacagawea, the Corps of Discovery's Shoshone guide and interpreter.

Bonaparte, Napoleon (1769-1821) - French Army officer who seized power after the French Revolution and in 1804 named himself emperor.

Clark, William (1770-1838) - U.S. explorer who, along with Meriwether Lewis, led the Corps of Discovery, well-known exploration of the Louisiana Purchase (1804-1806).

Lewis, Meriwether (1774-1809) - Secretary to President Jefferson and U.S. explorer; with William Clark, he led the Corps of Discovery in exploring the Louisiana Purchase (1804-1806).

Sacagawea (1788-1812) - Shoshone woman who served as guide and interpreter for Lewis and Clark during their exploration of the Louisiana Purchase (1804-1806).

York - William Clark's African-American slave and life-long companion, who accompanied Clark on the expedition. Clark granted York his freedom about 10 years after their return, and he moved to Kentucky.

TIMELINE

1682
French explorers in the Mississippi River valley claim an immense territory for King Louis XIV of France and name it Louisiana.

1763
With the Peace of Paris that ends the French and Indian War, France gives New Orleans and Louisiana to Spain.

1775-1783
The American Revolution wins the 13 British colonies their independence, the birth of the United States of America.

1800
Spain trades Louisiana back to France in the Treaty of San Ildefonso. Thomas Jefferson is elected President of the United States and serves until 1809.

1802
Spain's King Carlos IV officially transfers Louisiana to France. The Spanish administrator in New Orleans closes the port to American shipping.

1803
President Jefferson sends James Monroe to France to help Robert Livingston, the U.S. Minister there, attempt to purchase New Orleans. They succeed in buying all of Louisiana for $15 million. Congress ratifies the treaty in November.

1804-1806
Jefferson sends Meriwether Lewis and William Clark on an expedition called the Corps of Discovery to explore the northern and northwestern sections of Louisiana.

1862
Congress passes the Homestead Act, and by 1890 two million people have moved into the West and claimed land as provided by the Act.

REFERENCE

Modern map of the United States that shows the territory gained by the Louisiana Purchase.

● Louisiana Purchase

Historic map used by Lewis and Clark.

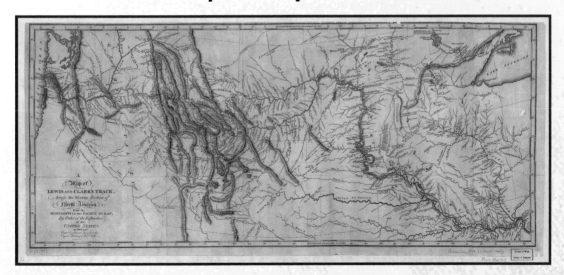

WEBSITES TO VISIT

geography.about.com/od/historyofgeography/History_of_Geography.htm

www.monticello.org/site/jefferson/lewis-and-clark-expedition

www.loc.gov/collection/louisiana-european-explorations-and-the-louisiana-purchase/about-this-collection/

SHOW WHAT YOU KNOW

1. In what year did Spain trade Louisiana back to France in the Treaty of San Ildefonso?

2. In what year did Thomas Jefferson send Lewis and Clark on the expedition known as the Corps of Discovery?

3. In what year did Congress pass the Homestead Act?

4. Name two of the species of animals Lewis and Clark discovered on their expedition.

5. Who was Sacagawea and what role did she play in Lewis and Clark's expedition?

GLOSSARY

bond (bahnd): a paper that represents money owed; a piece of paper sold to raise money that will be paid back in the future with dividends

celestial navigation (suh-LES-chuhl nav-i-GEY-shuhn): charting one's course by observing the positions of stars, planets, and other visible bodies in the sky

envoy (EN-voi): a person who represents one government in its dealings with another

Federalist (FED-er-UH-list): belonging to the United States political party formed in 1787 and led by George Washington

frontier (fruhn-TEER): a border between two countries; a region that is on the margin of developed territory

headwaters (HED-waw-terz): the source of a stream or river

interest (IN-trist): a charge for borrowing money, usually a percentage of the amount borrowed

interpreter (in-TUR-prit-uhr): one who interprets or translates for people speaking different languages

keelboat (KEEL-boht): a shallow, covered, flat-bottomed riverboat used for freight

mouth (mouth): an opening; the place where a stream enters a larger body of water

portage (PAWR-tij): the work of carrying or transporting goods, especially overland

ratify (RAT-uh-FYE): to formally approve

seaboard (SEE-bord): the country bordering a seacoast

secede (si-SEED): to withdraw from an organization or nation

successor (suhk-SES-ur): one who follows, especially one who takes over a throne or office

territory (TER-i-TOR-ee): a geographical area; an area under U.S. control with a separate legislature but not yet a state

INDEX